Shapes That Stay

Shapes That Stay

Poems by

Yvette A. Schnoeker-Shorb

© 2021 Yvette A. Schnoeker-Shorb. All rights reserved.
This material may not be reproduced in any form, published,
reprinted, recorded, performed, broadcast,
rewritten or redistributed without
the explicit permission of Yvette A. Schnoeker-Shorb.
All such actions are strictly prohibited by law.

Cover and book design by Shay Culligan
Cover photograph by Terril L. Shorb

ISBN: 978-1-954353-47-3

Kelsay Books
502 South 1040 East, A-119
American Fork, Utah, 84003

—For my husband, Terril, and all the other beautiful and inspiring
creatures with whom I feel blessed to share my life.
My muses know them well.

Acknowledgments

Many thanks to the following publications for being the first to give these respective poems a place to dwell.

200 New Mexico Poems: "The Tenth Child"
Blueline: "Birds and Atoms"
Chest Journal (American College of Chest Physicians): "Hippocrates Is Turning in His Grave"
Clackamas Literary Review: "Besting the Mouse"
Clockhouse: "My Husband Says I Need to Start Reading Novels Again"
Front Range Review: "Your Mother"
Green Hills Literary Lantern: "The Shadow of Our World"
Hawai'i Pacific Review: "Of Silk and Blossoms"
Medical Literary Messenger: "Waiting to Have Blood Drawn"
Peacock Journal: "Giving Thanks Before Dinner in the Present Progressive"
R.KV.R.Y Quarterly Literary Journal: "To Be Like Him"
Rockvale Review: "Diary Entry on the Run"
Sliver of Stone Magazine: "What It All Means"
So to Speak: A Feminist Journal of Language and Art: "Rocking Chair"
Spirit's Tincture: Speculative Fiction and Poetry: "In the Time of Spirit"
Split Rock Review: "Something for Her Dog"
Stickman Review: "Dreaming of the Dead"
Sulphur River Literary Review: "Kin (1930)"
Switchback Literary Journal: "Anything, Anywhere, Anytime"
The Midwest Quarterly: "Little Things"
Weber: Voices of the Contemporary West: "About Do-Not-Feed Signs"
Wild Earth: "Blue Winters of Reptilian Nature"

Contents

The Sister Who Never Was	11
My Husband Says I Need to Start Reading Novels Again	12
Dreaming of the Dead	13
In the Time of Spirit	14
The Shadow of Our World	15
Diary Entry on the Run	17
Blue Winters of Reptilian Nature	18
Of Silk and Blossoms	20
To Be Like Him	22
What It All Means	23
Hippocrates Is Turning in His Grave	24
Your Mother	25
Waiting to Have Blood Drawn	26
Besting the Mouse	28
About Do-Not-Feed Signs	30
Little Things	31
Kin (1930)	32
The Tenth Child	33
Birds and Atoms	34
Belonging to the Infinite	36
Giving Thanks Before Dinner in the Present Progressive	38
Something for Her Dog	39
Anything, Anywhere, Anytime	40
Rocking Chair	41
Shapes That Stay	42

The Sister Who Never Was

Last night she abandoned me
in a used-car dealership;

sometimes it's an airport,
other times it's a bus station.

With her, I never know
which glare-lighted site

will flare up in memories,
in nightmares. Alone I watch

my life placed in motion,
each isolated moment

crowded by others. Some
souls try to comfort me,

say my cruel, older sister
and I most likely

don't share the same DNA,
but how could they know

in the minutes and blood-
flooded tunnel between us

my twin had been stillborn.

My Husband Says I Need to Start Reading Novels Again

I just mailed my DNA to Portland
where a lab will determine once
and forever whether or not I have
a mutant gene; by chance or design,
with life so defined, I can't help
but wonder what innate sense
of fate drives this mind of mine
to know if somewhere there
dwelling in the center of my cells
with their chromosomes capped
by dutiful telomeres, within
those twisted strands hiding
and curled securely at my core,
a nucleobase is misbehaving,
adenine replacing cytosine,
messing up the sequence,
a repetitive impostor about
which there is nothing I can do.
My husband says I need to
start reading novels again
instead of science journals,
something less technical
that gives my thoughts a rest
from myself, but a protagonist
obsessed with her own matter,
I insist on unraveling this
story and even more so on
finding a fiction of perfection,
that is, unlikely detection
and existence unflawed
by a genetic liability.

Dreaming of the Dead

We are both dreaming of the dead
lately, you talking to a president,
I consulting a colleague; both
would have been good advisers

if they hadn't appeared as ghosts
of interest in breakfast conversation.
The oatmeal thickens, and the plot
becomes mushy, as does most

of the substance of dreams
turned sunny-side-up into narratives.
But how have we yoked ourselves
to the recurring presence of past

people haunting our thoughts?
I ask you what this might mean,
as you serve a plate filled
with toast to William Shakespeare.

In the Time of Spirit

We walk briskly, quickly weaving
among the slow-moving streams
of tourists, new-agers, culture-stealers.

"Really," I say, bored and now angry,
impatiently shaking my arm, noticing
my watch has suddenly stopped.

"Cheap piece of junk," I loudly hiss
to my husband, adding, "Next time,
I'm getting something good—a Rolex."

"So, we're at the Medicine Wheel,
and instead of spiritual things,
you're thinking about how you need

to get a new watch?" he questions me;
then a second voice, feminine, floats
into my ears like a feather on the wind,

"Yes, your watch stopped,
but if you don't respect the sacred,
next time it will be your heart."

I look around, behind, then down
to find the time piece on my wrist
has started working again.

The Shadow of Our World

The disappearance of shadows
finishes the day; twilight
slips through forest.
Watching constellations rise,
yearning to tear into the night,
to see what is behind that fabric,
I climb upward to a path
along the edge, ice sparkling
white beneath my boots.
Rhythmic violence sounds,
crunch, crash, crack, crack,
fresh, like the smell
of hunting season; a deer shoots
across the trail, her tail
vanishing into conifers.
Catching the ancient lunar orbit,
earth begins to darken the full moon.

Below the eclipse,
my town stands winter gently,
housed souls unaware of a changing face.
The sideways grin thinning,
leering, taunting, haunting
those who mourn
the loss of light. Curled
in a snowy clearing,
someone nearby is dreaming,
or I am. Chilled by the stillness,
my gloved hand meanders
over an orange vest to frozen lips—
no warmth, no moisture, no memory,
only a scent of the familiar

as chimneys below breathe blue
up to a crescent faintly glowing;
under this glimmer,
I feel the shadow of our world.

Diary Entry on the Run

Dried lilacs swell
like purple flame
crushed on paper,

a notebook, a pen,
the storm, deep in
wine—a pause, alone

here, the desert;
I'm floating
into almost night.

Hiss to the snake,
chatter to scorpions,
tell the dashboard rose

whose saved flesh
is the color of salsa
I won't be dancing

in darkness again
where clouds grow
low and growl

against a thinning
horizon, for I've had
too much scarlet

lately, and the stars
are starting to cry
tears onto my page.

Blue Winters of Reptilian Nature

When the chaparral blooms
greasewood yellow to pioneer bees
and ragged-winged butterflies, flutters
of orange in shadowed canyons,
they sleep, burrow-tucked,
rattles and tails, scales
and claws, jaws, and snouts
curled into barely breathing circles
beneath rocks, sheltered in roots,
lodged in layers of logs; outside,
in cool streams of sunlight,
the closest resemblance
to anything reptilian and alert
is the eye of a passerby
mockingbird perched atop a paloverde,
ash-hued head tilted and watching
suspiciously in silence
as I leave indentations
of identity, one foot after the other
crunching through the pink-grained
vein of wash bed.

I miss them in winter—the reptiles,
those quick motions or senses of shape
that signal, in warmer seasons,
the presence of a snake or tortoise,
whiptail, skink, Gila monster, or swift,
yet they still move,
not under this sad shade of sky,
but within the deepest part
of my brain, in crevices of gray matter
where forks in the desert

are never tongues of the living,
tips of organs sensing particles
floating in an arid breeze
above pebbled sand and shrub;
below, I rest in the substrate
somewhere in the complex path
between limbic system and cerebellum,
dreaming into their hibernation.

Of Silk and Blossoms

The silk pulses with them,
larvae, little gray strands, tiny lives
squirming, woven over the fragile stems
and first pink blossoms
of my apple sapling. Biased
toward the tree and fruit promised,
my heart is mute of reason
not to end the mass of worms, except
                                  I know,
dense as they are,
they, too, have as tenuous a hold
as any of us on life,
a vapor to still their nerves
or a gape-beaked chasm
form of fate.

Maybe it is the shimmering of spring leaves
                                  everywhere
or the sunburst butterfly wing
brushing one corner of the sky
that evokes blooms of irrational considerations.
Which new life gets expressed
in a season when the earth signals seductively
for all to come forth—worms or blossoms,
                                butterflies or apples?
Displacing life is risky;
with stick and conscience carefully tended,
I gently free the sapling,
moving the life it nurtured to a larger tree,
knowing that even riskier still

is the guilt of a meddler
who might fall under the scrutiny
of a god who finds yet another Eve
                                        tampering

with the process of creation.

To Be Like Him

To hell with the apple—at her core,
Eve simply wanted to explore paradise
before converting it to Eden.
But she sought advice
from the problematic tree—the only tree
that would ever cut down a human.

Yet the scarlet, fertile fruit seduced her
as knowledge is hot and once inflamed
the sassy lass snaked her way to Adam;
with each kiss, offered her hypothesis
on why she so desperately desired
the mind of the creator.

I know how she felt,
for the fateful flame was
not the type one holds for a lover;
still, it glows with want, blue
in the center with sin-red heat
inspiring the heart into submission.

But it is the psyche that fans the fire
and which designed Eve's descent—the fall
rendered as a consequence of some savage
angel extending his residence from heaven
to earthly woods, rather than being depicted
as merely a woman's addiction to theory.

Clearly, how could Eve's craving forbidden
frameworks hidden in that hot-bed garden,
that is, her heady attraction to abstractions
sired first by some admired other,
be portrayed as depraved or as betrayal
when it feels so much like love?

What It All Means

My blood sugar is on the rise,
but out here in the badlands
the antelope still run freely
across uneven earth
beneath a cloud-mottled sky;
nothing is perfect.

I watch, somewhere between
appreciation and scrutiny,
anticipating the sharp bite
from a hungry mosquito
positioned on my arm.

Go ahead and dine
on my fine blood
defined by its dangerously
glorious glucose. Drink up,
my tiny, whining friend—
nothing is perfect.

Hippocrates Is Turning in His Grave

The first time I went to a specialist,
he had me—naked from the top up,
sheeted from the breasts down—
lie on the examining table,
where he felt hand to skin
every organ in my body. He was
from the "old school" of medicine,
more efficient than robotic,
less impressed with technology
than he was with patient cases,
but the hospital replaced him
after he turned eighty.

So when you tell me how
your new, young gastroenterologist
didn't even have you undress
but simply discussed your condition,
chronic stomach ailments, I wonder
if she failed you, all those possible
parts of you crying out for attention,
to be felt, to be understood
by someone whose tactile sense
was trained by tradition, not by
a current practice in medicine
that eliminates touch.

Your Mother

"Beware of bears,"
she warned before I left
to walk the badlands
a few feet from her ranch
in Wyoming; now,
in the distance, that blur
could be anything
in the late summer dusk,
but everything comes
to mind when alone
and vulnerable—
bloody skulls, lipless
screams of hikers
attacked on some trail,
or the black bear
you told me about
punching a bag of plums
strung between pines,
sharp tips of claws
ripping the twine.
But your mother
has warned me
about bears or wolves
for over a decade now
whenever I wander
outside, and I fear
her concerns
have clearly now
become mine.

Waiting to Have Blood Drawn

She doesn't seem stressed.
We have in common blood,
that and a dread of the draw
for which we impatiently
wait in the sunlit room
with cookie-cutter chairs
and green—philodendrons
everywhere; my god,

the waiting area is being
re-wilded. The corner
once contained a tiny aviary
with frightened little birds
soon replaced by a large
aquarium with frantic fish;
they're gone, and that space—
the entire place—now drips

with new nature, prolific
plants, strands of heart-
shaped foliage overflowing
from hanging pots; leaves
stream from the ceiling,
curl around paintings,
fall onto magazine tables,
gentle life everywhere,

unaware of the screaming
flat screen—infomercials,
televised pharmaceutical-
ese, pleas for us to pester
our doctors when blood
betrays us with abundant
expressions of ailments. Still,
she doesn't seem stressed,

the elderly, well-dressed
woman wearing earplugs;
rather, she appears intense-
ly interested in one specific
robust plant, pulls a small
scissors from her purse: snip,
snip, snip, clip, and she walks
out quickly with the cutting.

Besting the Mouse

Why do they have to be so clever
when they trespass, assertive and smug,
seeing me as nothing more
than a supplier of succulents
to quench their thirst
in territory without water?

I know he is napping comfortably
somewhere in this house
as I pick up the needle-toothed remains
of my plant, bits of green still oozing,
strewn around the terra-cotta pot;
tiny droppings nearby mean nothing,
so ubiquitously placed
that trails can't be traced.

To best me, I'm sure,
nature made him nocturnal; I hear
that percussion body thumping
rhythmically as he jumps
from cupboard to counter to floor,
scampering throughout the night,
inviting contempt. I should buy a trap—
one of those effortless, disposable kind,
sticky, one that catches the mouse
by his scratching, clawed paws
and, when panicked and pupil-eyed
he begins to gnaw,
that sharp, quiver-whiskered nose.

I would find him in the morning,
nimble movement gone,
tantrum-tailed and stuck, waiting
to be trashed—alive.
But how could I discard
the value of a breathing, warm, heart-
beating thing.

About Do-Not-Feed Signs

Okay—they *are* wildlife,
but they know us so well;
long after the signs have fallen
and humans are not around
in Yellowstone, these ravens
will be here, and their generations
to come with blood-red gapes
beckoning, squawk-screaming,
wings flapping, begging for morsels,
more bits of bread, cookies, crackers,
whatever we all fed them illegally
because their eyes and cries
were irresistible, and our deep
inclination could not be overridden
even when forbidden.

Rising above geysers, engulfed
by fog forming on the lake—
serene and steamy, the dark
and dreamy, sharp gaze
of ravens will still gleam
with intent to glean
as the young continue to follow
from stones that once defined
a now vacant parking area
to the other side of the road,
where they will drift in and out
of holes across in crumbling cliffs
to share with their parents
the eggs of hysterical swallows.

Little Things

There is nothing here
but little things,
pointed aster shadows
dotting gray earth,
clusters of spiderlings
riding on their mothers' backs,
ants building pebbled monuments
to be abandoned in floods,
and locusts, colors snapping shut
with the click of each landing,
little things that fly and crawl
and breathe in the heat
moving through soft hills
that roll into the distance;
we giants also breathe,
heavy, little breaths,
our footsteps cracking
brittle badlands clay
as we share
that state of smallness
so relative to place.

Kin (1930)

for Willis Jones

Yellow moon midnight high,
full and faintly moving
above August fields, corn dense,
sloping to our pasture fence
and Brown Swiss tied,
still, one eye open,
cow listening with expectation
to quick steps, barefoot walking,
two sisters softly stalking,
skin to husks, silk within—
whisper, whisper,
swish, swish, swish,
young hands brushing leaves aside,
through rows at night
naked figures gently glide,
emerge with pails glimmering
at the edge of hard times.
Silent, hidden nearby, Uncle and I
crouched in dark greenness
on damp earth; uncovering
the mystery of missing milk,
we continued to go without
during those mornings
deep in the Depression.

The Tenth Child

Her mother told her
that the birth of the atom bomb
occurred before the daughter was born,
and it happened secretly
when they were tent dwellers
waiting to build a house;
exposed to the black blanket of sky,
they were not used to seeing
                        daylight at night.

After that time, it took ten tries,
miscarriages or stillborns,
to have a baby. This daughter
was the first one born alive
                        who stayed alive—
although later siblings suffered
deformities from fallout.

Testing now is no longer done
without warning. It doesn't take place
only in "uninhabited" areas
of the New Mexico desert
but within the vast space
                        of her body;
so far, everything is normal,
but sometimes in a dream
                        her soul explodes.

Birds and Atoms

Once she leaves her shell,
the vulture knows
those zones of orbits
closest to the earth,
that grounding nucleus,
are filled
with the motion of other birds,
so she seeks the bluest
layer of flight spectrum.

Like an energized electron
circling the edge
of some outermost orbital,
she waits to interact
with the gods
or at least be pulled
to the invisible heavens
of a less negatively charged
other world.

But she never crosses
the spheres,
for there is no ionic bridge,
and no covalent sharing
of her and another,
to bond the two worlds.
Even with all that energy,
her release is still
a downward spiral.

Birds and atoms,
vultures and electrons—
everything is motion;
when the wings
complete the final flap,
atoms untrap
themselves from each cell,
electrons flying
to more attractive forms.

Belonging to the Infinite

I am concerned about dying,
so we take a table way in back
where he attempts to comfort me
with the first law of thermodynamics:
Energy can neither be created
nor destroyed. It can only change form.
As my biggest fear, after that of pain,
is that I will get lost before
I find a path leading to heaven,
he suggests there is no such place
and no hell, simply infinity—and God
everywhere and for eternity.

Ranch, thousand, house vinaigrette . . .
At the table next to us everything
is on and the server offers a choice—
unlike the option of immortality,
and I wish this distraction would move
to the other side of the restaurant
or, even better yet, the universe.

So now I feel compelled to confess,
a whisper, I am still concerned
about transformation, loss of memory,
loneliness in a vast space, no sense
of place, not having family or friends,
and again, pain, particularly before
the change, when I am still aware
that I am dying. But he reassures me
about my continuance on a journey,
claims I will always exist as one
form or another because we all
belong to the infinite.

Blue cheese, balsamic, honey mustard—
Is it really that complicated? The course
of life, I realize, is not a salad;
yet, now I am concerned
that once I belong to the infinite there
may be no such thing as greens.

Giving Thanks Before Dinner in the Present Progressive

Thank you, Lord, for this food
we are about to receive,
my cousin offers as we hold hands
and bow our heads; I try to hide
my chewing, swallow my first bite
quickly, hoping no one notices
I forgot to first give thanks, am not
in the habit of doing so at all.

My cousin overlooks the obvious,
catches my eye, judges me neither
as glutton nor ingrate; instead,
having practiced patience, she
gives me an understanding glance,
smiles, and begins again,
Thank you, Lord, for this food
some of us are presently receiving . . .

Something for Her Dog

She is quite serious, the woman
at the counter in front of me,
when she asks the clerk,
"Can you recommend
something for my dog? He's
allergic to animal products."
I turn my face away to avoid
being seen about to burst
into laugher and pretend
to focus on a selection
of nearby cat toys.
Puzzled but straight-faced,
the man responds to her,
in a noble attempt
to appear sympathetic,
"If you mean vegan dog food,
we only have vegetarian."

I know nothing about dog food,
nor do I care—I prefer birds,
wild birds, feeding them only
the best, which is why I am
picky about bird seed. And
the twenty-five-pound bag
I am holding is getting heavy.
Oblivious to other customers,
the woman continues
to chat, asking the clerk
to assist her in finding recipes
for homemade dog food.
When she finally leaves, I drop
the bag down on the counter
and ask, "Is this bird seed
certified gluten-free?"

Anything, Anywhere, Anytime

A poor passenger, I'm not
inspired by this window view,
hills, rivers, pastures, cows, flowers,
fields—scenes that will outlast me.
But passing quickly by the glass,
filling the frame, a red and yellow
wall with thick, bold, black words,
Anything, Anywhere, Anytime,
appeals to us bored mortals
living life in the slow lane,
inconvenienced by transition,
ultimately by death. Now that's
a message inclined to capture
my immediate interest; it is
the hopeful promise of control
at my fingertips, the consoling
pledge that before the downward
edge of my existence, all the needs
of my brief and fragile lifespan
can be fulfilled by my very will.
It's all mine—*anything* I want,
anywhere, anytime. Whatever
the actual cargo carried and aside
from solicitous slogans, the sign
gracing the side of that truck
racing by is the first thing
on the road I've seen all day
on which my attention is sold.

Rocking Chair

Is there room for me
                     in the ground?
An old woman who needs
to go home,
I am not willing to uproot
yet another flower, blade of grass,
beetle, earthworm—
I'd rather sit here quietly, brittle
hair electric, lips colorless,
whisper-breathed, shady eyed—
windows closed, body
                     rocking
back and forth, feeling rhythm
in the turning of memories;
settled into slow motion, soul
floating an ocean of space,
                     I rock,
caressing the oaken arms
of my tomb,
with no place left
from which to leave
                     this world.

Shapes That Stay

Where the elk had been standing
grass doesn't sway, dandelions
refuse to be bent by wind,
and a shadow of the cow
remains still—she remains
in yesterday, watching me pass
forever. Some call this memory,
but what if the resonance
resides in the air, in nature itself?

I fill the same motion
that propelled me into today,
each step a little stray
from the day before and before
that even as the same she-elk
now walks by straight ahead
to graze in the meadow beyond,
both of us creating our paths
into the shape of tomorrow.

About the Author

Yvette A. Schnoeker-Shorb's poetry has appeared in many publications, including *Weber—The Contemporary West, AJN: The American Journal of Nursing, The Midwest Quarterly, High Desert Journal, About Place Journal, Front Range Review, Medical Literary Messenger*, the anthology *Talking Back and Looking Forward: An Educational Revolution in Poetry and Prose* (Rowman & Littlefield Publishing Group), *Terrain.org: A Journal of the Built and Natural Environments*, the Jungian journal *Depth Insights, Sonora Review*, and other journals and anthologies. She holds an interdisciplinary M.A. from Prescott College and is an educator, a researcher, and an editor. Using their trademarked survey, The Kellert-Shorb Biophilic Values Indicator, she, her husband, and a small group of colleagues are currently investigating the multifaceted and often seemingly contradictory ways in which humans in the U.S. perceive and relate to the natural environment. She is co-founder of the 501(c)(3) nonprofit natural-history press, Native West Press.

www.ingramcontent.com/pod-product-compliance
Lightning Source LLC
Chambersburg PA
CBHW021028090426
42738CB00007B/943